Messages To The Heart

Carol C. Ernst

Published by Leadership Horizons LLC

317-844-5587

888-262-2477

Carol@leadershiphorizons.com

$ 9.95

Copyright©2003 By Carol C. Ernst

*In Loving Memory
of
My Brother
Scott Culbertson*

I wrote Messages to the Heart
during a three month period in late 2001.
After my morning meditations
I began hearing words
which formed the poems found in this book.
Each morning I received two or three of these poems.
I didn't understand the poems at the time.
I questioned why I was hearing them, what to do with them,
And how and why it was happening.
I did realize though, my "thinking" halted the creative process.
I encourage you to experience my poems
In the same way I received them: read a poem,
Meditate, and receive its unique message to your heart.

I learned to trust this process and allow God to use me.
Putting myself in God's hands
I experienced that God can and does use us in
mysterious ways.
My prayer for YOU is:
God, use my mind to think through,
My mouth to speak through,
And set my heart on fire!
These messages are now for your heart.
Blessings,
Carol

Messages For a Healing & Awakening Heart

I am a chosen channel
for words of wisdom
to touch all who desire to know.
I am grateful
my heart and mind connect
allowing the words of wisdom to flow.

Blessed are the changing times.
Blessed are those
who bring the energy
that directs the change.
Hearts sing
as your energy glows.
All opportunities and possibilities
are within you.
Those of light awaken.

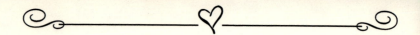

Messages for Healing

My soul has the eyes of God.
Tears of joy and sadness flow openly.
The joy of life
also brings sadness for the dead.
But joy comes again
as we remember
we are all alive in God's eyes.

I know your eyes speak for your soul.
When I look in your eyes
I can hear you in ways
that can't be explained.
See the soul's of many
as you look into the eyes
of all you encounter.
Then bless each soul
with your own eyes.

Lights sparkle in the sky
but lights also sparkle on earth.
What do stars see
when they look at earth?
Your thoughts of love, joy and peace
create a light that sparkles.
Someday we will see this sparkle
that the stars already see.

Filling our hearts with love and joy
is not what we were taught to do.
We need to learn how to open our hearts
like windows
and find love and joy on earth
in things we see, hear, and feel.
We ask this joyful sensation to join us in our hearts.
Then we can take this with us
and share it with all.

My dear Mother Earth,
remove the sadness
that fills my heart.
Transform the sadness
into love and joy.
Then teach me to share this
as you do
the fruits of your bounty.
Blessed be my Mother Earth.

We heard you crying.
We caught your tears.
We heard you praying
and answered your prayers.
It's with your own heart
that lives are touched.
So give of your heart
and the circle of peace
begins
again and again and again.

Here Hear Here
So many tears.
It is time to let love flow
into the tears
and hope floats into your heart.
There it blooms into a flower of God.
Water the flower
with the love of tears.

It is a time of healing.
Hearts are filled with tears.
Only hearts that are filled with joy
Can touch the tears.
So please,
the many,
begin to find the joy in life
and share it with those
whose hearts are full of tears.

"Why" will never be answered for you
There are always
many answers to why.
Let go and release "why"
and fill your mind with "it is".
Now your heart
can finally do it's job of healing
since it no longer needs to argue
with the mind's question
"Why"?

Pray for the dead who are still alive.
Pray for the living who are now dead.
Let go of the burden and feel the pain.
Allow the healing
to replace the sorrow.
Remember the dead are alive
and so also are the alive, alive!

Healing is flowing,
Sense the flow and step into it.
It feels like a stream
with an occasional rock.
Water flows over and around the rock
it never stops.
You too will flow around the rocks.

Healing is wholeness
and wholeness allows God
to have an even closer relationship
with you.

When will the pain end
and the healing begin?
The pain is the healing
so you've already begun.
When does it end - the pain?
Maybe when we realize
that pain is the scar tissue
that heals our wounds.
When we deny the pain
we deny our own healing.
So allow the pain
and know you are healing.

Many times I've cried your name out
to nothing and no one
There was never an answer
as you had left this earth.
One day an answer came
when I called out your name
for the 100th time.
You said, "I've never left you,
I'm here right now
can you finally hear me?
I've answered every time you called
but you never **believed** until now."

When will I join my loved one again?
When will I hear
the laughter of their being?
It is already happening
so be thankful always
that you can hear
your loved ones laughter
alive in your own heart.
Laugh with them until you join them.

Gently I left the body
to sit in the heart of God.
Here I felt the peace
and love and healing
that the great one offers me.
Then,
I accepted it
and felt a joy
as pain and sadness
was lifted away.
Light as a feather
I drifted back to my body,
transformed by the love
of God's healing heart.

Why must our hearts feel pain?
Pain can create a larger heart
which then allows more love
to flow into the world.
So accept pain
as an exercise
to strengthen your heart
so it can pump more love.

Time

The message is becoming louder.
Can you hear the ticking of time?
It is nearing our hearts desire.
Many hearts will fill with love
and peace.
Silence is not reality.
Singing hearts can be heard
when we use our soul to listen.

Make time, make room, make love
a priority in Life
and you will then know true joy.

My My the times seem rough
Can I have another view?
Yes, now I see a time of joy
that is already beginning to grow
from my soul's desire.
It's a beautiful flower for all to enjoy,
That's me!

Hear Ye Hear Ye Hear Ye
Arise, awaken and be joyful.
It is the Golden Age.
Alive now, and be at peace
for all who have chosen are here
to know the love of God
Within themselves.
Bless you.

It isn't how much or how many

Instead it is were there any?

Times you felt the presence

of a higher power.

It is always around you, open up.

Falling water filled
with messages for many.
No one hears the water talking to us.
What might it be saying.
Live and love many, always.
There is not enough time
but there is still tomorrow
Use everyday for enjoyment.

Another time another place

We are always in time together.

Forever is the time it is right now.

It's a time of joy and wonderment
for those who know
the change is coming.
Soon they will understand
what must be realized by many
and will take their places as decided.
Allowing the change
to flow into your heart
will direct you
to your place with ease.
Never and forever is now.

Isn't it funny how things come and go?
People are the same way.
We are always coming and going
in some form or another.
How do you know
when it's time to go?
How do you know when to come?
Is there a sign
that tells us your time is now,
or does our soul
know how to read
this coming and going time piece?

It is what is. There is no not.
Coming is going
and leaving is coming.
There is always a full circle.
It is the time of now
and many hear this message.
Eyes ears and hearts
awaken the rest of our soul.
To the treasures that are ahead of us.

Here it is a time of joy.
Listen to the music
of a heart filled with joy.
It is also a time of sadness,
hear this heart music also.
Is there a difference?
Of course not,
joy and sadness
are played the same way
and both are from the heart.
So why are many crying
when the music of the heart
is both joy and sadness?
The tears are for themselves
and the ones they think
they have lost,
but they haven't.
This is why the music of joy and sadness
are the same.

If it isn't now then when.
When it's tomorrow it's too late.
If I can't see the light
does that mean it's night?
Will my soul ever
come out of the dark in time?
How is a question
that always is answered
When how is not answered
we believe there isn't a way.
How can we awaken the
hearts of so many?
Any way you can.
Help is on it's way
Don't be sure
until you see it.
If we wait to "see" the help
we might miss it.
Especially, if what we are looking for
doesn't look like
what we think help will look like.
So how will I know?
Only the hearts eyes will recognize.

It is the time of Light
please listen to our words
and fill your whole being
with this energy of peace.
Peace can only be found
in our own hearts.
Find peace with yourself,
your family, and then your world.
Know that peace
feels like acceptance then joy.

How beautiful are the lights
that fill the sky at night.
Only with the darkness
can we know this beautiful sight.
Thank you for the darkness
so you could show me light.

Open hearts of love and Light
fill the world with joy.
Open yours to love and light
and listen to the music now play.
Blessed is the world when it is filled with singing hearts.

Hearts

Blessed are the "I am's"
full of life and joy.
Take none for granted.
Hear the music of hearts everywhere.
Rejoice with the beating of each one.
Open your heart
for the music to flow in and out.

This is a time of unrest
Hear the bells.
Listen closely to your own heart.
It is speaking to you now.
Joyful Joyful Joyful
This is the time
your heart has been waiting for.
So open your heart
to God's energy of love and peace
Then spread it.

Silently loud

sound the bells of change.

Quietly listening our hearts respond.

Awakened by tragedy

or was it?

Now is the time of light and dark.

But can there be only one?

Acceptance is our hearts desire.

This is a time of changing hearts.
Hear the echo of a voice
in your own soul.
As it becomes louder and louder
you will not be able to ignore it.
Ask the voice to come into your heart.
Then listen to its musical guidance.

There are many who have awakened
To the dull beating of their heart.
It soon will become the music
in their lives.
Listen and converse with the wisdom
that lies in the music of your heart.
Play the music now and
let the music play you.

Keep on writing

the head and heart scream.

Keep on writing

the words pour

through the instrument.

Am I the instrument

or is the pen the instrument?

Maybe we both are?!?!

If humans express themselves

with a pen,

does God express himself

with humans or through creation?

If so, how do we know!

If we know, how do we let that happen

or does it just happen?

Keep on writing

the head and heart scream.

Here is how messages
pass through the ages.
So here me say.
Hear then say.
Hear with heart.
Say from the heart.
All is not known with our minds
but is known with our hearts.
Allow your heart to show you the whole picture.

Many have risen
to the sound of the times.
You are here now
to awaken ready hearts.
Hold your own energy of love
in your heart.
Allow it to beam a path ahead
for you to follow.
Teach all who come to you
to see their hearts path.
Bless YOU!

Help me know
what words to use
to touch the hearts of many.
Even tho the words
cannot fill the empty hole,
they can heal the relationship
between myself and God.
I hold onto the words
even tho they are not God.
They are the comfort
that can come from God.
Thank you God.
The words help me to know
you are there.
Then I begin to see you in the wind
and the falling leaves.
In the light of the day
and the dark of night stars.
Then I hear you in the birds that sing
and the rush of water.
You're here now all around me
and I'm so glad to know that.
Thank you for words.

Memory is the first to go
and first to come back.
So remember who you are.
It is not who you may have "thought " you were.
It is now
who your heart
has always known you are.
Celebrate the seed of your being.

Where does the whisper
of your voice go
when you die?
What happens
to the beat of your heart
and the blink of your eye?
Is it lost forever
or has it gone someplace else?
Maybe it's a memory
that remains alive in my own heart.

Light

Instantly it happens
That our hearts begin to change
When those around us
feel our new energy of love
Celebration happens in the heavens.

There seems to be a spell
that has come over the land.
It's the fluttering of hearts
as they awaken to a new dawn.
Excitement is finally replacing fear,
and faith grows deep within us
anchoring itself in our souls
and attaching to life in the moment.

Heavens doors are opening now.
Many hearts connect
to those hearts in the heavens.
Allow this energy of love
from both sides
to fill the spaces & places
on Earth.
Thank You.

Hear the sun the moon and the stars
Do you know what they say?
They sing and dance
with silent words of music
for all to hear.
Listen again.
They are whispering the words
of a harmony
that says,
Light and Dark can harmonize
for all to hear and see.
Be at Peace then Be Peace.

May the world be at peace.
May the world's heart
fill with love and light.
May the world
and all of its beings awaken.
May the world recognize its wholeness.
May the world
spread the energy of love
to all beings on Earth.

He She are merely descriptions
of gender.
There is no gender in the afterlife.
Allow yourself to see men & women as humans.
Now you can see equality
in all people.

Hope

Hope is not as strong as faith.
Hope is a flicker, faith is a flame.
Flame into the world of you
knowing there is no wind
ever strong enough
to extinguish you.

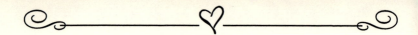

Abundance

Plenty is everywhere.
Plenty is abundance.
It is flowing to and through
your hearts.
Pictures of plenty
already exist in your hearts.
Get them out,
look at them and know
you create them.

Handfuls Handfuls Handfuls
More than we can know
Hallelujah Hallelujah...
Now is a time of sharing handfuls.

Soul's Journey

What is it?

I do not know.

Who is it?

I'm not sure.

Can I touch it?

Why not.

What is a soul?

What is it not? Is it a person?

Is it a heart?

Where does it begin and end?

Does it live & die?

Do only people have souls?

Can I see a soul?

How?

I'm not sure.
But I'm quite sure.
Has it happened yet?
I think so.
Don't think, know.
When you allow yourself to just know
then you don't have to think anymore
and you will act out of wisdom.

Happiness ends, joy does not.
Forever is longer than for now.
Will is our connection to God.
Choice is use of our will.
It is a joy to forever be filled
with the will of God.
That's my choice.

Why must I die?
Why must I live?
Know that the choices
were made long ago.
Accept your part
know it fits you.
Just as the leaves
fit on the tree
so does your life
fit on the Earth.
Nothing dies and all is alive
with an energy of some form.

Hello Hello Hello
Is anybody there?
FOREVER there is a knocking
on the door to your soul
or is it?

Feel the presence of a power
that is unseen.
Ask the presence to heal
all your life's sorrow.
Allow this energy
to release
any negativity that fills your heart.
Be grateful
for the healing presence
of God.
Amen

Now is the time of change
and you are to be a part of the change.
Many more can feel the heartbeat
of Mother Earth speed up
as she begins to birth
a new consciousness here on Earth.
One that fills the planet
with Love & Joy always.
Bless and keep the heart
of our mother
in our own hearts.

When will this be? How will we know?
Are there more to come?
Who is in charge?
Patience, love, wisdom
Allow these to fill your heart
knowing you need no answers
for transformation to happen.

Joyful are those
who find beauty in each day.
Wise are those
who can appreciate themselves.
Fear is not present
in these hearts and minds.
Allow God to dissolve your fear
so once again
you can enjoy yourself and the day.

It's done but never over
It has begun but never ends
Blessed Mother
who is always in our hearts,
may your smile fill the void
we feel
in our lives apart.
May your eyes
always share your wisdom
and may we always trust
our own eternity.

Help is always around and within you.

Call upon it now.

Rest assured

that it will arrive in time

for you to know who you are today.

God spoke to me one day
and woke me from my sleep.
The words were loud
but his love was louder.
I felt God in my soul.
I'm grateful for the presence
of God
in the home of my soul.
What a welcome guest.

Have you ever wondered why?
What happens
when you wonder why not?
Is there a difference?
Isn't one questioning "what is"
While the other questions
"the possibility"?
Which one will allow
my spirit to grow larger…
That's the why I want.

Isn't it silly what is.
I can't quite tell what is and isn't.
So why bother trying to figure it out.
Just know one is and isn't
forever.

Isn't it funny how things turn out,
what if things turned in?
Why do we say how things turn out,
what does turn have to do with it?
Aren't we always turning
here on earth?

So what can I tell you
that you don't already know?
And if I told you
would it make a difference?
Is it good or bad?
You already know
all you ever need to know
so listen to yourself and KNOW!

Forget and remember
is a cycle you know.
Forget and remember
the people you've known
and the people you've been.
Someday,
forgetting
will not be a part
of your makeup anymore.
Instead you will just remember.

Hasn't it always been true?
Can you understand?
Forgive and forget
can be as long as a heart releases.

Hearts are filled with the joy of plenty
More will know the feeling of love
for the time of heart is here now
and love will flood the planet.

Isn't' it always the same
or is it always different?
The way we seem to see
the things
in front of us.
When we begin to see something
that was always the same
as now different
will be the time
we have been waiting
for- forever.

How can we ever know

what is really real?

How can we know what isn't real?

How do we measure

real versus imagined?

Is it our own minds

that create real versus imagined?

If so, can we also choose

which one we believe?

Is that faith or folly?

Carol Ernst

Partner, Leadership Horizons, LLC
You may contact Carol at 317-844-5587 or carol@leadershiphorizons.com

Carol is a Partner with Leadership Horizons. She specializes in coaching, team building and personal effectiveness programs with a particular emphasis on building productive, effective and satisfying working relationships. She is also the lead facilitator for their company's RealTime Coaching™ training program.

Her work with individual clients helps them discover their heart's desires and experience it through their work. Her tools are compassionate personal dialog and insightful self-awareness building profiles. The awareness Carol stimulates in her clients may surface deep personal beliefs that are blocking growth and development. Through skilled dialog she helps her clients begin making the changes they seek in their lives.

She is a reiki healer and is trained in the Pilgrimage healing process™ which she uses in her local church, St. Luke's United Methodist. She has been involved in the Spiritual Life Center at St. Luke's since it's inception, and currently serves as its Chairman.

Carol has had a variety of experiences both in for-profit and not-for-profit organizations. Her business experience includes being an apparel buyer for L.S. Ayres and a Designer and Sales Associate for Corsi Cabinets. As a Marriage and Family Therapist she has worked in private practice and as an outpatient therapist in the St. Vincent's Health Network.

Carol has a BS in merchandising and an MS in Marriage and Family Therapy both degrees are from Butler University. She is also a Certified Professional Analyst in behaviors, values, and attributes by TTI Performance Systems, Inc.. She lives in Fishers IN with her husband Ron, her business and life partner. They both have a desire and intent to help others by learning and growing, beginning with themselves.

Thank You.